I0476008

THE
RESPONSE
AGENCY
GUIDE
TO
DIRECT
MAIL

What works
What doesn't
How to get started

Steve Cuno
Chairman and Founder
RESPONSE Agency, Inc.

© 2017 Steve Cuno. All rights reserved.

No part of this book may be reproduced, stored in a retrieval system, or transmitted by any means, electronic, mechanical, photocopying, recording, scanning or otherwise, except as permitted under Section 107 or 108 of the 1976 United States Copyright Act, without the prior written permission of the authors.

While the author has used his best efforts in preparing this book, he makes no representations or warranties with respect to the accuracy or completeness of the contents of this book and specifically disclaims any implied warranties of merchantability or fitness for a particular purpose.

ISBN: 978-1-304-75079-2

Contents

Chapter 1

Good Direct Mail Earns a Profit

Since you're reading this guide, you're probably a marketing decision-maker. Due to that fact alone, you probably receive a lot of junk mail. Chances are you toss most of it, unopened, into the trash.

So it's only natural to ask if direct mail really works.

The answer is an unequivocal YES. Every industry you can name uses direct mail to retain, grow, and cross-sell to existing customers, and to add new, profitable customers. In addition, smart marketers use direct mail to predict a campaign's outcome and profitability *before* backing it with big dollars.

Yet most companies don't do direct mail as well as they could, and get dismal results as a consequence. Why? Usually it's because they're unaware of the vast body of knowledge about proven direct response techniques available to them.

So, for starters, here's your first, big direct mail tip: *Take the time to learn what works. Then trust it, and use it.*

The RESPONSE Agency Guide to Direct Mail is a concise summary of best practices. The secrets you're about to learn have emerged as consistently effective and reliable, based on not just years but on decades of ongoing testing.

This is probably a good time to bring up a few definitions. *Direct response, direct mail,* and *direct response mail* are often used interchangeably. But indulge me in getting technical for a moment.

Direct response is the craft of getting a market to respond directly back to the advertiser. It isn't limited to direct mail. Direct response techniques exist for email, TV, radio, print, digital media, and outdoor. Although this guide focuses on *direct response mail*, you can adapt what you learn here to other media with great success.

Direct mail is anything you happen to mail to lots of people. Companies that send out a lot of mail but don't employ proven direct response techniques are technically doing direct *mail*, but not direct *response*. Which usually means they're not getting the results they could get if they did it right.

Direct response mail is the most specific term. It means you're sending out direct mail that employs proven direct response techniques. It is the smartest, most profitable way to use the U.S. Postal Service, and it's what you're going to learn how to do by reading this book.

Chapter 2

What's a "Good Response"?

A question that often comes up is: *What's a good response? Is it 1%? 2%? 3%?*

It's a trick question. Successful direct response marketing isn't defined in percentages. *A good response is one that achieves break-even or better, regardless of percentages.* A good response leaves you in the black after you've paid for your list, printing, mailing, and postage.

When you're promoting a product or service, calculate the expected Lifetime Value of a new customer. Suppose that, on average, you earn about $500 over the life a customer relationship. If you target 75,000 prospects and spend $50,000 on printing, mailing, and postage, you'll need to win at least 100 new customers to break even. Expressed as a percentage, that's about 0.14%. But if a customer is worth only $25 in profits over a lifetime, you'll need about a 2.7% response to break even.

So, in the former scenario, a "good" response is 0.14% or higher. In the latter scenario, a "good" response is 2.7% or higher.

The question that usually follows is: *What response should we expect?* This is not a trick question, but it's still a tricky one. If you have a product or service that is often sold via direct mail, you should be able to track down past response rate data and use it to inform your expectations. If you want to sell credit cards, for instance, it will be helpful to know that direct mail credit card offers historically pull between a 0.4% and a 0.6% response. But always remember that no two products, creative approaches, or sets of market circumstances are alike. Your own credit card offer may fall outside the norm. The only way to *know* what to expect from your mailing is to conduct valid test mailings. (See Chapter 7, "How to Track and Improve Results.")

It's important to agree with management on what constitutes a *good* or *successful* mailing *before* you begin. If you're fortunate enough to attain a 0.28% response when 0.14% marks the break-even point, the last thing you need is management overlooking a spectacular two-to-one ROI and expressing disappointment because response was "*only* 0.28%."

Do not let yourself or your management get hung up on percentages. Percentages matter only to the extent that they relate to profitability.

Chapter 3

Three Steps to Successful Direct Mail

Creating direct mail is fun. It's tempting to hop right in, dream up headlines, and imagine how your mailer will look.

Resist.

The appearance and content of your direct mail are important, but first you'll need to do a little homework. Otherwise, you risk creating beautiful, creative direct mail that misses the mark.

Follow the steps below in order. Resist the urge to skip ahead, or you'll end up with a cart ill-suited to your horse.

Direct Mail Step #1

The first step to creating successful direct mail is: *Know where and how to reach your market.*

Knowing *where* to reach them will help lead you to a reliable mailing list. Knowing *how* to reach them will help you connect mentally and emotionally—that is, *empathize*—so your message will be relevant. To do that, you'll need to know how they think, and what matters to them.

When direct mail yields disappointing results, failure to properly target and empathize with the market is the top reason. I'll discuss reaching and connecting with your market in detail in Chapter 4, "Smart Targeting."

Direct Mail Step #2

The second step to successful direct mail is: *Give people a compelling reason to act the moment they receive your message.*

It's not enough to "get your name out there." People need a reason to act and act now. Sorry, but your good name and stellar reputation aren't enough. The best marketers go one step further, and I'll show you how in Chapter 5, "The Big, Huge, Important Rule That Never Changes."

Direct Mail Step #3

The third and final step to successful direct mail is: *Use proven copy and layout techniques.*

Creating copy and layout is the part of the direct mail process that many people enjoy most. That's where they get to show off a little creativity. Caution is advised. Thanks to the measurable nature of direct response marketing, there is a vast body of knowledge about kinds of techniques that work, and kinds that don't. Writers and designers should learn them before setting to work, in order to better inform their creativity. I'll go over the basic techniques in Chapter 6, "25 Response-Building Secrets."

Chapter 4

Smart Targeting

If you're already imagining what your direct mail will say and how it will look, stop and back up.

Successful direct response mail begins with smart targeting—and that means *understanding your prospective buyer, along with his or her point of view.* This accomplishes two important goals: (1) It increases your odds of finding the right mailing list. (2) When you write, your work will be relevant and compelling.

Getting to know your market

An overall starting question is: *Who is likely to buy what's for sale?* Resist quick conclusions like "We're selling to adults who own cars." You can do better.

Basic demographics help. What is the age range of your prospects? Income range? Where do they live? Will your product interest women, men, or both?

Now, challenge the assumptions you just made. *How do you know* the age, income, neighborhoods and sex of your market? Do you really know, or did you assume? Maybe you should look through your database, ask your customer contact people to share observations, visit with customers, or hang out in your store and discreetly observe who your customers are and what they do. You may be surprised at what you didn't know, and at what you may have incorrectly assumed.

Next, get to know your *profitable* customers. (Remember that your highest-spend customers aren't necessarily your most profitable ones.) Since it's not unusual for businesses to break even or lose money on 80% of their customers, trying to appeal to *everyone* is unrealistic as well as an unwise way to spend your marketing dollars. It makes more sense to focus your direct mail on retaining and growing profitable customers, nudging almost-profitable customers toward becoming profitable, and seeking new customers from among people who bear a demographic and psychographic similarity to your profitable customers.

Having determined basic demographics, it's time to get to know your customers better. What makes people want what you're selling? What matters to them? Why? Do they tend to be conspicuous or conservative when it comes to showing wealth? What drives them? What worries them? How do they vote? Do they have relationships with your competitors? What do they like about some of your competitors and dislike about others? Are they self-employed? What do they read? Do they watch TV? When? And what do they watch?

Some of these questions will prove unanswerable, but the questions that you *can* answer will lead to useful insights. Better still, they will help turn your focus from *what you want to say or sell* to *what interests your customer.* Both will increase your odds of a successful direct mail effort.

The best mailing list

The best mailing list available to you isn't available to anyone else. It's your own customer list. Direct marketers call this a *house list.* Since your existing customers know you, they are more likely than anyone else to open and respond to direct mail from you. If you've already organized your customer files into a database, good. If not, start now. If you haven't been collecting and sorting customer names and addresses, start now.

You can use your house list to: 1) identify, retain, and grow best customers, 2) grow borderline customers into profitable ones, and 3) offer incentives to your best customers for referring friends and associates.

Mailing list essentials
(Three questions to ask your list broker)

Besides your own customer list, a number of commercially traded lists are available. A good list broker can help you with recommendations. Since not all marketed mailing lists are created equal, here are some questions to ask a list broker to increase your odds of obtaining a reliable one.

FIRST QUESTION: What is the source of the list? Mailing lists of people who have already responded to a mail or online offer have obvious advantages. These are called "response lists," and they tend to be well maintained and up to date. They comprise only people who have responded to a mailed offer, which means they're more likely to respond to yours. You can select lists of people according to the *kind* of offer to which they responded, and by how recently they responded to it. For instance, if you want to sell women's sweaters, you can obtain lists of people who bought women's clothes, or even just sweaters, in the past 30, 60, or 90 days via mail.

You can also order *subscription lists*. For instance, to target small-business owners, you might mail to people who subscribe to magazines about small business; to reach young parents, you might mail to people who take parenting or children's magazines. Be sure to select and test carefully. People often move without updating their subscriptions, so the list may not be as up-to-date as some. And be careful not to assume that a magazine title offers a perfect picture of its readers. For instance, a given travel magazine's subscribers may do more dreaming about travel than actual traveling.

Compiled lists are exactly what the name implies—the product of digging through records and directories and copying down the information in them. The compiled information is only as good as its source and its copyist, and there is no guarantee that the source was accurate or up to date or that the copyist was meticulous. This is not to say that all compiled lists are to be avoided. A skillful list manager will refine and update the list and turn it into a quality product. A lazy one won't. How can you tell which kind you're dealing with? See the second and third questions, which are coming up in a moment.

You're not limited to one list. It's often a good idea to rent a representative sample of names from several lists, and test them all at once. Chances are you'll find that some outperform others. It's reasonable to assume that the remaining names on the successful lists will produce as well as the sample.

You can also overlay lists. For example, to attract diving enthusiasts for high-end scuba products, you might overlay diving magazine subscription lists with financial data lists.

SECOND QUESTION: *How is the list verified?* If you learn that the manager of a list regularly updates it after mailing to it, qualifying it by telephone, or both, that's a good sign. If the list manager simply compiles data without verifying it regularly, beware.

THIRD QUESTION: How often is the list updated? Addresses change faster than you might think, so the more often a list is updated, the better. Ideally, a list should be updated at least quarterly. If it's updated only semi-annually, that's OK too. Annually? Only as a last option. If it's never updated (or the answer to "How often is it updated?" is "I don't know"), don't waste your money buying it, and especially don't waste your money mailing to it.

Other tips – When a mailing list is available for rent, not for purchase, it can be a sign of a well-maintained list. If you intend to mail to it more than once, be sure to negotiate multiple uses in advance. (List managers know when someone reuses a list. That's because the list includes just a handful of their own agents at various addresses. You, of course, don't know which names and addresses these are. When one of those agents receives your mailing, they know you used their list.)

If a list manager requests a sample of what you intend to mail, don't take exception to it. In fact, appreciate it. It means you're dealing with a company that won't allow just any offer to go to its lists.

The U. S. Postal Service maintains a National Change of Address File (NCOA). For a nominal cost, you can update any list by running it "against" the NCOA file. Always a good idea.

The Direct Marketing Association (DMA) maintains a voluntary, national "Do Not Mail List" of people who have asked *not* to receive direct mail. Ask your list manager if they have removed those names from the list you're about to use. If not, visit *www.the-dma.org* and request the list for yourself, so your letter shop can purge the names.

Many companies maintain their own "Do Not Mail" and "Do Not Call" lists. It's an important customer courtesy to honor these requests. It also spares you the needless expense of mailing to people who'd rather not hear from you.

Chapter 5

The Big, Huge, Important Rule That Never Changes

Let's deal with the reality of human inertia.

If your company is well regarded, your products are terrific, and your customers are loyal, that's wonderful, but it's not enough to get people to act on your direct mail offer.

People put things off. Most of the time, no matter how relevant your product offering, and no matter how creatively you present it, even interested prospects are likely to set it aside, never to return to it. Worse, many more people will discard your mail unopened with hardly a glance and forget they ever saw it.

Good news: there is a proven way to overcome human inertia, to increase the number of people who promptly respond to your offer instead of postponing it for a someday that never comes, and decrease the number of people who consign it unread to the trash.

Which brings me to the big, huge, important direct response marketing rule that never changes.

It has no exceptions.

None.

If you learn nothing else from *The RESPONSE Agency Guide to Direct Mail*, learn this rule. It's that important.

Here is the rule:

THE WAY TO GET THE MOST PEOPLE TO RESPOND TO YOUR DIRECT MAIL IS TO OFFER A COMPELLING, LIMITED-TIME, FREE INCENTIVE.

THERE IS NEVER AN EXCEPTION TO THIS RULE.

NEVER.

Here's an example: "Sign up for a Home Equity Line of Credit within 30 days and we'll thank you with a free Samsung tablet." Here's another: "Enroll this month and we'll send you a $100 Bed Bath & Beyond gift card, free." And so forth.

If you recoiled and gasped, "No, not *that*," I understand, and you're not alone. Most people react that way—at first. But when our doubting bank client tripled checking account upgrades with a free flashlight offer, our forms printer client doubled sales with a $10 Victoria's Secret gift card offer, our gas fireplace client increased response 20-fold with a $1 jar of honey offer (I'm not making that—or any of this—up), and our respected, private liberal arts college client increased applications for their MBA program fourfold with a $25 gift bookstore gift card offer—well, let's just say we made believers out of them.

In a nationwide test for a service industry category leader, we found that changing the creative work—even the brand name—had no effect on sales. None. What *did* have an effect? Adding an incentive offer.

A dramatic increase in response to the right incentive offer is the rule, not the exception.

An incentive offer gives you a major strategic advantage. Embrace it.

Fallacious objections to free incentive offers

Once you embrace big, huge, important rule that never changes, expect objections from your boss or your boss's boss. Over the years I have and debunked them all repeatedly, so perhaps I can prepare you.

The most common objections are "This is unprofessional," "It's an insult to our customers," "We shouldn't have to bribe our customers," "Our customers won't respond to a gimmick," "We can't afford to give things away," and the ever popular but equally fallacious "Our clients are too intelligent to fall for that."

In fact, they're all fallacious. Let's dismantle them one at a time.

FALLACIOUS OBJECTION 1: *"This is unprofessional."* If that's true, then American Express, General Electric, Honda, DeBeers, Steinway, Chase, Mercedes-Benz, and a host of other companies are unprofessional, too. These and other equally respected companies use free incentive offers as a matter of routine.

FALLACIOUS OBJECTION 2: "It's an insult to our customers." Only if an inept writer makes it sound insulting. When you ask people to reply promptly to your mailing, there is nothing insulting about thanking them with a token of your appreciation.

FALLACIOUS OBJECTION 3: "We shouldn't have to bribe our customers." What you should or shouldn't have to do might make for an interesting (though more likely a tedious) philosophical debate, but this isn't a philosophy book. It's a book about what makes the most people respond to direct mail. The dismal response of direct mail *without* an incentive offer and the continued success of direct mail *with* one says that, yes, you *do* have to bribe your customers. If it makes you feel better, replace *bribe* with *motivate.*

FALLACIOUS OBJECTION 4: "Our customers won't respond to a gimmick." We replaced *bribe* with *motivate,* so let's now replace *gimmick* with *incentive.* Having dispatched the prejudicial terminology, we can better examine the claim that your customers won't respond to an *incentive.* Actually, they will. Or, rather, significantly more of them will than would if you omitted the incentive offer. The free incentive offer didn't become an industry standard because it doesn't work.

FALLACIOUS OBJECTION 5: "We can't afford to give things away." Of course you must choose an incentive easily covered by your margin. If your margin is $20, do not give away an incentive that costs you $30. Duh. With that understood, trading an incentive for a dramatic increase in sales sounds like a pretty good deal. Moreover, *high perceived value* needn't mean *high cost*. For instance, a booklet with valuable information can be highly prized yet cost little to print. A free latte motivates, yet costs a pittance.

To ensure that an incentive falls within a realistic budget, start by calculating the Lifetime Value of your average customer. That is, what can you expect, over how many years, to receive in profit from a new customer? Subtract your overhead. Now you have a good idea of what you can afford to spend on your mailing in general, including the incentive. If the numbers show that you'll need an unrealistic response to reach break-even, you may need to come up with a less costly incentive, rethink your strategy, or challenge the viability of your product.

FALLACIOUS OBJECTION 6: "Our clients are too intelligent to fall for that." For one thing, experience shows that *the wealthier and more educated the customer, the more an incentive offer increases response.* For another, no one is trying to get anyone to "fall for" anything. The simple fact is that truly intelligent customers are more likely to respond when there's something extra in it for them. It's rather an intelligent thing to do.

As your incentive offers pay off, expect jealous competitors to envy your success and accuse you of not playing fair. I suggest you receive the epithet, as my clients have. Take it as a sour grapes-motivated, backhanded compliment, all the way, as Liberace once said, to the bank.

Chapter 6

25 Response-Building Secrets

Direct mail results are measurable. Thanks to that, there is a wealth of information about top-selling direct mail techniques. Observe the following tips, and you will be well on your way to direct response success.

1. *Remember your objective.* When you begin work on copy and design, it's tempting to be distracted by an urge to create something cute, clever, entertaining, memorable, arresting, or sure to win an award at your industry's next marketing conference. Which is all fine, except if you allow those things to become priorities, your original objective—presumably, that of generating a sale or an inquiry—can end up lost in the shuffle. Contrary to what most advertising agencies allege, creativity alone does *not* ensure results. Creativity is an important tool. But sound selling techniques and relevance come first.

2. *Limit choices.* Too many choices tend to make people decide *not to decide at all,* meaning that you lose the sale. Your product may be available in a choice of 20 colors with six different sets of features and in two sizes, but your mailing must present no more than three options, period. Even catalogs with hundreds of items limit the options for each to three (like "good-better-best").

3. *Pattern your direct mail after the best salespeople.* Think about the successful salespeople who call on *you*. Chances are they dress and groom themselves appropriately, present features and benefits in a clear manner, and seek to close or advance a sale. But what if they took a radically different approach? What if they dressed unprofessionally, regaled you with wisecracks and awful puns, named the product three times, and left? If you answered that such a sales approach would repel rather than win business, you're right. *Yet that is not unlike the behavior of much of today's so-called "creative" advertising.* Don't put out stuff like that. Your direct response mail needn't be dull, but it must avoid what bad salespeople do, and emulate what great ones do.

4. *Use an envelope, and make it work hard.* Your envelope has one job: to make people open it up and eagerly dig in to its contents. There are many ways to make an envelope more enticing. For instance, you might try making it look like personal mail, or displaying a compelling headline (perhaps featuring your incentive offer), or using an unusually big or unusually small envelope, or featuring an unusual window.

5. *Don't use mailing labels.* A mailing label screams, "I'm mass-produced junk mail—throw me away!" Use a laser or ink-jet printer to address envelopes. Handwritten addresses may increase sales somewhat, but the added time, labor, and risk of error may increase your cost by more than your gain.

6. *Enclose a killer sales letter.* A solid sales letter is of top priority in direct mail. It is more important than any other enclosure, including brochures and flyers. Writing a sales letter is not job for amateurs. If you cannot hire a pro, study and imitate what the pros write.

7. *The letter should <u>look</u> like a letter.* Use a legible font. Have a salutation. Have one (and only one) signature, preferably in blue.

8. *Enclose a business reply card (or reply form with a courtesy envelope).* Despite the convenience and availability of the Internet and telephones, a significant number of people still respond by mail with a business reply form, and many complete the form before calling or going online. You may not need to use postage-paid cards and envelopes. Some marketers find that response actually increases when customers supply their own postage. I can't explain that one, but I accept the numbers that back it up.

Many people set aside the reply form for later action and discard the rest of the envelope's contents, so be sure the form has a brief summary of your selling proposition and incentive offer, with your phone number and URL prominently displayed.

People like to check boxes, so be sure to put a box next to the word YES that your respondent can check. The box will not diminish response and may increase it. Don't put a shadow behind the box, don't fill it in with a color, don't put a check mark in it, and don't make it any shape but square.

If you're requesting sensitive information such as account numbers, Social Security numbers, age, income, etc., provide a reply *form* along with a reply *envelope*. To provide better security, be sure that no one can see through the reply envelope.

9. Consider adding a brochure. Brochures are useful for showcasing an item for sale, or for displaying a gift incentive offer. A brochure can also legitimize your brand, and restate or add to the benefits in your sales letter. In some cases, a good brochure will increase response; in others, it will only add cost. You should test your direct mail both with and without a brochure. If the brochure fails to increase response, there's no sense spending money on it. Leave it out.

10. Consider adding a lift note. A lift note is a small, folded note that adds one more push to the sale. It might contain testimonials, a closing thought from the marketer, or showcase an incentive offer. Like a brochure, it *may* increase response, and should be tested. Omit it if it fails to pull its own weight.

11. Or skip the whole letter-and-envelope thing and send a postcard instead. Letters reigned supreme in direct mail until digital media came along. The rising generation is growing up less acquainted with letters-in-envelopes and more acquainted with the likes of social media, chat, tweets, email, and text messages. That gives direct mail an advantage: young people like getting mail and notice it because it's unusual. But with the cachet of letters and envelopes pretty well lost on them, a less costly-to-produce postcard may serve. As a general rule, the bigger the postcard, the better.

12. *Make responding easy.* No matter what you mail, display your phone number and URL so that people who aren't even looking for them will nonetheless see them. That means make them BIG. As a general rule, if your art director doesn't complain, they're too small. Putting a telephone icon like ✆ next to your phone number will increase the number of calls you receive. If your boss or art director tells you it looks tacky, agree and do it anyway.

13. *Be clear and to the point.* Busy people don't take the time to eke meaning out of an enigmatic headline. It's better to be straightforward. If your incentive offer is a free iPod, the headline "Free iPod with your purchase of ..." requires less thinking on the part of your busy reader than "Think of this offer as music to your ears." Though arguably less creative, the more direct headline is likely to produce greater response.

14. *Motivate.* Don't just *describe* your products and services. Present them so that people will *want* them. Even a checking account can be interesting. You must walk a fine line here. Hollow raves fail to convince, and too-clever writing calls attention to itself instead of to the benefits you're offering. On the other hand, you cannot bore people into buying. When you're *honestly* convinced that you have a great product, let your conviction shine through in your writing. If you're not honestly convinced, you need either to dig deeper into the product until you see the light, or to admit that your product or incentive offer is lackluster. In the latter case, you may need to rework the product, or change your strategy to give greater emphasis to the incentive offer.

15. *Say neither more nor less than enough.* Don't be afraid of long copy. If it's well written, it will probably sell more than short copy. Still, be sure to edit out everything you don't need. Copy should be long enough to do its job, and not a word longer. Or shorter.

If your objective is to generate leads, your copy should be on the shorter side. The idea is to say only enough to create interest and induce your reader to request more information. If you're trying to complete a sale, you'll need to tell readers everything they'll want to know in order to make a decision.

16. Don't obsess over what doesn't matter.
Never mind if you would prefer the word "pleased"
where your writer used "happy," if you think "act now"
is more positive than "don't delay," or if you'd prefer a
green accent color instead of blue. Nitpicking at that
level of detail usually has little or no effect on response,
while it demoralizes writers and artists and wastes
time and money. Evaluate creative work from a big-
picture perspective. If it's getting the job done, leave
the fine-tuning to the fine-tuners—your writer and
layout artist. (If someone photocopies this paragraph
and leaves it, unsigned, on your chair, consider it a
hint that someone thinks you're a nitpicker. If you
find yourself tempted to rewrite this paragraph, you
are a serious nitpicker.)

17. Use conversational language. Never mistake
stuffy, impersonal language for *professionalism*. It is
the opposite. The most educated reader appreciates
short words, simple sentences, and a personal touch.
Never say "ingest" or "masticate" when "eat" or "chew"
will do. Never say, "We wish to show our appreciation
for the long-term nature of the relationship we
have with you as a client," when you can say, "I
noticed you've been with us for a number of years.
I'm writing to say thank you." And while *I'm* on the
subject of conversational English, *don't* be afraid to
use contractions. *Or fragments.* And be assured that
sometimes a preposition is just the thing to end a
sentence *with.*

30

18. Use a serif font in sales letters and brochures. You can use sans-serif fonts like this one online, in headlines and subheads, and on postcards, but avoid them in letters and brochures. Serif fonts (like the one this book is set in) are easier to read. "Easier to read" means more people will read it (that is, fewer people will give up on it), and "more people will read it" means you'll sell more. *Why* people find serif fonts easier to read remains a matter of debate. And, with sans-serif fonts as the de facto digital media standard, that may change.

19. Set body copy with dark type on a light background. Reversing your type (light letters on a dark background) reduces readership. I don't recommend putting a color or photo behind body copy, but if you must, go for high contrast so that type remains easy to read.

20. What you say matters more than how it looks. The most engaging layout won't save writing that fails to persuade.

21. But how it looks matters. The first thing people do upon receiving direct mail is *look at it.* Make sure your piece creates a relevant and positive first impression.

22. Layouts should be accessible. Besides making a good first impression, a layout's job is *to support the selling proposition.* Be sure readers can instantly tell where their eyes should start, go next, go after that, and so on, all the way to your call to action. Speaking of which …

23. *Include a clear, easy-to-find call to action.* Even when your copy shines and extols the virtues of what you're selling, you're not finished. Urge people to respond on the spot. Don't be afraid to say, "I urge you to call now, because the free flash drive offer expires in 30 days," or, "Why not respond now, while it's on your mind?" Place the call to action where a reader who isn't looking for it will find it anyway.

24. *Track responses.* You'd be surprised at how many marketers neglect this important step. Make sure you have a leakproof system that counts all responses—phone calls, clicks, hits, personal visits, and business reply cards. Follow those responses all the way through to closed sales. Only then will you know when your program succeeds, and by how much.

25. *Avoid all-or-nothing thinking.* The techniques presented here will greatly increase the likelihood of a successful program, but they cannot ensure it. Chances are your initial response will please you, but if early results are lower than you'd hoped, don't scrap the program, and don't discount the power of direct mail. Evaluate, adjust, and try again. More on how to do that is next.

Chapter 7

How to Track and Improve Results

Direct response marketing is empirically measurable. People either respond or they don't. For marketers, this feature yields three significant benefits:

1. You can identify and quantify successes.

2. You can defend your program from bean counters when they turn a greedy eye on your budget.

3. You can improve results without increasing your budget.

All of those things will make you a hero in the eyes of your management and board of directors. But in order to pull that off, you'll need to be able to track direct response results—and figure out what the results mean.

Basic direct response tracking

Let's say you mail a direct response package to sell a dog training course to dog owners. There are four ways people may respond: online, by mail, by phone, or, if you have a store, in person. How do you track results?

For those who respond by mail, tracking is easy. If you enclosed a postpaid business reply card that is specific to this direct mailing, you will need only count the postcards that people mail back.

For online replies, you'll need to direct customers to a special landing page. If your URL happens to be *XYZCompany.com,* create and direct them to *XYZCompany.com/dogtraining.* Then it's a simple matter of counting visitors. Once they register and request information, they should be able to click from the landing page to your main site.

For telephone replies, asking callers where they saw your offer has its limitations. People don't always know what sent them to the phone. It's not unusual for people to say they saw a TV or newspaper ad, even when there aren't any. A better method is to set up a unique phone number for exclusive use in your mailing, and then count the calls made to that number.

If you're worried about the rigmarole of setting up extra phone lines, there's a simpler solution. For a surprisingly low cost, you can lease a unique phone number from a specialized vendor. All calls ring at your location as usual, but the vendor's computer system counts them. The vendor can also tell you how many calls you missed (useful for spotting staffing or training issues), record calls so that you can monitor quality, and provide a list of callers (useful for follow-up).

So, there's no reason you can't have a precise count of mail, online, and telephone results.

Some people will respond to your direct mail in person, that is, by walking into your store. As with phone inquiries, asking walk-ins how they heard about your offer is not reliable. Here are two solutions: (1) Enclose a coupon in your direct mail package that walk-ins must bring with them to redeem an incentive offer; and (2) compare a list of walk-ins to your original mailing list. Neither measure is precise. People forget to bring coupons, and good customer relations demands providing the incentive anyway; and walk-ins may have missed the direct mail and shown up on their own. But, against the backdrop of mail and telephone replies, these two measurement methods will at least provide a gauge.

Secret weapon: your control group

Sooner or later, someone will look at your response rates and say, "How do we know we wouldn't have sold that much anyway, without the mailing?"

Do not preemptively dismiss this person as a curmudgeon. It is a valid question, and the answer matters. If sales would remain the same with or without direct mail, you would be well advised to find other uses for your direct mail budget.

How to know? Easy. When you send out your direct mail, always set aside a small but representative, randomly selected sample of people on your mailing list and *exclude them from the mailing*. These people are your *control group*. Once results are in, compare the percentage of respondents who received the mailing to the percentage of respondents from your control group, who didn't receive it. If both groups purchased at the same rate, your mailing had no effect. If the control group purchased at a lower rate, you can safely assume that your direct response mail is doing its job, and that the sales you attained would *not* have happened on their own.

Not even the cagiest bean counter can argue with solid control group data.

How to keep improving results

If you sent out a direct response mailing, measured results, and calculated the Lifetime Value of the resultant business vis-à-vis your marketing objectives, good for you. You now know whether your direct mailing succeeded. That's a big step. You also know that you can expect about the same response every time you mail the same package to additional names from the same list.

Still, all you know is whether your mailing performed. What you don't know is how it might have performed *better.*

The solution is to create *two* versions of the mailing, split your list, and send one version to each half. Suppose you create one version with Headline A and another with Headline B. If the Headline A version pulls a 1.0% response and the Headline B version pulls 1.25%, you know that Headline B is stronger. Flukes can happen, so it's usually a good idea to repeat the test. If the results hold, give up Headline A for Headline B. You will increase results by 0.25% *without increasing what you spend.* Management will love that. So will the bean counters, though perhaps grudgingly.

Suppose you want to mail an offer to 50,000 people and want to know which incentive offer is strongest. Select 6,000 random names from your mailing list. Create two versions of your direct mail, the only difference being the incentive. Send one version to one-half of the 6,000 names, and the other version to the other half. Track responses. In a few weeks, you'll know which incentive is more effective. At that point, you can "roll out" the winning incentive to the entire list.

There's no need to stop there. You can take your winning headline or incentive and test it against *another* one ... and test *that* winner against yet *another.* Over time, either you will continue discovering new, more powerful strategies ... or you will know that the one you're using has earned its place as the reigning champion.

This method, called A/B split testing, can reveal dramatic differences. Sometimes they are small, but often they are significant. I have seen A/B split testing produce differences in response as great as 800% or more.

You can use the A/B method to test anything. Headlines, creative platforms, layouts, colors, taglines, logos, pricing, you name it. Just remember to test *one* variation at a time, keeping all other elements identical, or you won't know what caused what. For instance, if the headline *and* photo in Version A differ from those in Version B, there will be no way of knowing whether a difference in response is due to the headline, the photo, or both. If you must test two sets of elements, you can, but you'll need to separate your mailing into four cells.(Two sets of changing elements means four permutations, each of which must be isolated for tracking.) In order to track response-by-version, each version will require its own phone number, landing page, and business reply card.

(It *is* possible to test multiple variations at the same time by means of Multivariate Testing. This requires large quantities and sophisticated analytics and algorithms beyond the scope of an introductory guide.)

What to test, in order of priority

You may remember from Chapter 3 that the steps to a good direct response strategy are, in order of priority:

1. Know how to reach your market.

2. Give people a compelling reason to act the moment they receive your message.

3. Use proven techniques in copy and layout.

It follows that you will have the greatest impact on your direct mail success by first testing to find the best-performing mailing list. You will have the second greatest impact by testing to find the best-performing incentive offer. Once you have learned all you can in those two areas, start testing different creative approaches.

It's a good idea to make ongoing testing a part of your direct response program. Even after settling on a winning approach, continue reserving a small sample of names from every mailing so you can test variations. You never know when a new approach will surprise you by beating the previous winner.

Chapter 8

Five Steps to Getting Started

Congratulations are in order. You now know more about direct response mail than most marketers in general. And, for that matter, more than most advertising agencies.

If you're wondering how to get started on your own rock-solid direct response mailing, here are five suggestions:

1. Identify a direct mail opportunity. You *could* ask what you want to sell, and who is likely to buy it. Better yet, approach the question from the other direction. That is, ask who your key market segments are, what they want, and what your company offers that will satisfy that want. Next, engage your IT folks or a good mailing list broker and find out how to reach the right people. If two or more mailing lists emerge as strong possibilities, send a test mailing to a sample of each. Then, compare results.

2. Conduct a mini-feasibility study. Calculate the Lifetime Value of the average customer you hope to attract. Next, calculate the cost of your proposed direct mail program. From there, it's an easy matter to figure out the response you'll need for your mailing to reach the break-even point. If the response appears attainable, proceed.

3. *Choose incentives to test.* Remember that an incentive must have sufficient perceived value to motivate action, but must also be considered as part of your overall budget.

4. *Create your direct mail.* Follow the guidelines in Chapter 6. If possible, create a couple of test versions. Remember to include unique phone numbers, landing pages, and uniquely coded business reply forms so you can tell which responses come from which version.

5. *Keep going.* Direct response isn't magic, and you shouldn't have unrealistic expectations. But because direct response is the only truly measurable form of advertising, it can give you a firm handle on what works, what doesn't, which strategies to roll out and repeat, and which to drop. Even your failures will prove instructive. The more you work with direct response, the more your direct response acumen will grow.

If you retain a direct response professional—which I recommend—avoid branding agencies that list "direct mail" or "direct response" as one of many capabilities. Direct response is its own discipline, not an adjunct. It requires bona fide expertise.

If you're interested in mastering the craft yourself, let the expert know. A good direct response professional will cheerfully coach you, even if it means working himself or herself out of a job.

About the Author

Steve Cuno is the founder of the RESPONSE Agency and the author of the books *Of Marketing and Emasculated Goats: Advertising and Marketing Insights from the Oddest Places*; *Prove It Before You Promote It: How to Take the Guesswork Out of Marketing*; and *"It's Not About the Sex" My Ass: Confessions of an Ex-Mormon Ex-Polygamist Ex-Wife* (by Joanne Hanks as told to Steve Cuno).

Steve is a popular speaker at conventions for the American Bankers Association, the Direct Marketing Association, the American Advertising Federation, the National Postal Forum, the James Randi Education Foundation, and colleges and universities.

You can call Steve at 801-971-0045, email him at *steve@responseagency.com,* or visit *www. responseagency.com.*

The
RESPONSE
Agency

To contact the RESPONSE Agency call

801-971-0045

or e-mail steve@ResponseAgency.com

For free articles and other useful information, visit
www.ResponseAgency.com

www.ingramcontent.com/pod-product-compliance
Lightning Source LLC
Chambersburg PA
CBHW021941170526
45157CB00005B/2375